CHRISTMAS
Holiday Grab Bag

by Judith Stamper

illustrated by Dana Regan

Troll Associates

METRIC EQUIVALENTS

1 inch = 2.54 centimeters
1 square inch = 6.45 square centimeters
1 foot = 30.5 centimeters

1 teaspoon = 5 milliliters (approx.)
1 tablespoon = 15 milliliters (approx.)
1 fluid ounce = 29.6 milliliters
1 cup = .24 liter
1 pint = .47 liter
1 quart = .95 liter
1 pound = .45 kilogram

Conversion from Fahrenheit to Celsius:
subtract 32 and then multiply
the remainder by 5/9

LIBRARY OF CONGRESS CATALOGING-IN-PUBLICATION DATA
Stamper, Judith Bauer.
    Christmas holiday grab bag / by Judith Stamper; illustrated by
Dana Regan.
        p.   cm.
    Summary: Discusses the origins of various Christmas customs and
suggests activities for the holiday season.
    ISBN 0-8167-2908-5 (lib. bdg.)   ISBN 0-8167-2909-3 (pbk.)
1. Christmas—Juvenile literature.   2. Christmas decorations—Juvenile
literature.   [1. Christmas.]   I. Regan, Dana, ill.   II. Title.
GT4985.5.S73   1993
394.2'68282—dc20   92-13226

Contents

Christmas Is Here!

What is the most popular holiday of all? The answer must be Christmas! No other holiday is so full of gifts, decorations, good food, and fun. At Christmas, we celebrate the love shared by families, the joy of living, and the hope of peace on earth.

Many symbols of Christmas — flickering candles, burning yule logs, evergreen decorations — have an even longer history. For early people, they were symbols of light and life in the midst of the cold winter.

Each country in the world has its own special Christmas customs. In America, such traditions were brought by immigrants from many lands. From the Germans, came the Christmas tree. From the Dutch, came Santa Claus. From the English, came Christmas caroling. The food, decorations, songs, and customs of many peoples have combined to make our Christmas a very merry holiday.

This book contains recipes, crafts, facts, jokes, and projects based on Christmas traditions. Share them with your family and friends. Together, you can spread the spirit of Christmas this year.

The Christmas Tree

The Christmas tree is a beautiful symbol of this season of light. From the White House to your house, the twinkling tree brightens the holiday.

Did You Know?

Christmas trees were first used in North America by German settlers. During the early 1800s, trees were decorated with candles, fruits, cookies, and ornaments. The custom spread across America and Europe during the nineteenth century.

When Thomas Alva Edison invented the electric light bulb in 1879, the future of the Christmas tree became even brighter. By 1907, electric lights on strings were made. Soon Christmas trees sparkled with lights in many North American homes.

Fir trees are used as Christmas trees because they are evergreens — they remain green all year round. People of long ago believed evergreens stood for life, and had the magical power to stay alive during the cold winter.

Each year, a huge tree is put up at Rockefeller Center in New York City. The tree towers above an outdoor ice-skating rink and twinkles amidst the skyscrapers around it. The city of Toronto, Canada, lights a huge Christmas tree in front of City Hall. In Washington, D.C., the President of the United States turns on the lights placed on the tall spruce on the White House lawn.

Christmas-tree farms provide most of the evergreens sold at Christmas time. Approximately 34 million trees are sold in America each year. The top choice is the Scotch pine. It is followed in popularity by the Douglas fir, the white pine, and the balsam fir.

Mistletoe is an evergreen plant with white berries. Long ago, people collected it during winter. They believed it had magic powers. An old Scandinavian legend started the tradition of kissing under mistletoe. The custom is still with us today!

Christmas Chains

What is colorful and long and brings Christmas cheer? A Christmas-tree chain, of course. Invite your family or friends to make these decorations with you.

Chains are an old-fashioned way to trim a tree. Popcorn and cranberries are used in traditional chains. Pasta and candy chains can add color and good taste to your Christmas tree.

To make each chain, you will need a darning needle (or a needle with a large eye) and heavy thread. Begin by making a big knot at the end of your thread. Then start stringing.

Popcorn

String popcorn on your chain. If one breaks off, eat it! A popcorn chain on an outdoor tree makes a nice Christmas gift for the birds in your yard.

8

Popcorn and Cranberries

Alternate popcorn and cranberries for a bright, red-and-white chain.

Pasta

Choose a type of pasta that has a hollow center to put a string through. Elbow macaroni and rigatoni are two examples. First, use food coloring to dye the pasta red and green. When dry, string the pasta pieces in a chain of Christmas colors.

Candy

Use Christmas candies in brightly colored wrappers. Tie knots around each candy and leave about an inch of space between each piece. Remember, don't eat until Christmas!

Popcorn Snowballs

Ornaments you can eat are a special Christmas treat. Use red ribbons to hang popcorn balls from the branches of your Christmas tree. They look like snowballs and taste terrific.

You Will Need

- 8 cups popped popcorn
- 1 cup granulated sugar
- 1/2 cup water
- 3 tablespoons white corn syrup
- 1/4 teaspoon salt (plus some from shaker)
- 1/2 teaspoon white vinegar
- 1 teaspoon vanilla extract
- Butter

- Heavy medium-size saucepan
- Candy thermometer (or cup of cold water)
- Large heatproof bowl
- Wooden spoon
- Plastic wrap
- Red ribbon
- Potholder
- Measuring cup and spoons

Steps

1. Ask an adult to help you prepare the popcorn. When it is popped, pour it into a large bowl. Salt lightly.

2. In a saucepan, mix together the sugar, water, white corn syrup, salt, and white vinegar.

3. Attach a candy thermometer to the side of the pan.

4. Ask an adult to help you heat the syrup in the saucepan. Set the saucepan over medium heat. Stir the syrup until all the sugar dissolves.

5. Bring the syrup to a boil. Let it boil until the thermometer reaches 290°F. (If you don't have a candy thermometer, test the syrup by dripping it from a spoon into a cup of cold water. When the syrup forms a hard ball in the water, it is done.)

continued...

6. Turn off the heat. Add the vanilla extract to the syrup and stir.

7. Using a potholder to carry the saucepan, pour the syrup over the popcorn. Mix it together well.

8. When the mixture is still warm, but not hot, rub your hands with butter and form the popcorn into balls.

9. Wrap the balls in squares of clear plastic wrap. Tie off the gathered ends with red ribbon.

10. Trim your tree with popcorn snowballs. You'll always have a present ready when a friend visits you at Christmas.

A History of Santa Claus

He goes by many names around the world. In England, he is called Father Christmas. In the Netherlands, he is Sinterklaas. In Russia, he is Grandfather Frost. We know him as Santa Claus.

This kind, jolly gift-giver visits children at Christmas time in many lands. Each country has its own story about him, for he is a mysterious fellow who arrives at night in secret. Here are some legends about him from around the world.

The very beginning of Santa Claus goes back to the fourth century in what is now the country of Turkey. A very kind and famous bishop named Nicholas lived there. Because of his good deeds, the people made him a saint when he died.

The legend of Saint Nicholas spread across Europe in the next centuries. He became known as the gift-giver. In the Netherlands, Dutch children would set out their wooden shoes on the eve of December 6th, the birthday of Saint Nicholas, in the hope that he would fill them with gifts.

When the Dutch settled in North America, they brought their holiday customs with them. Saint Nicholas was pronounced "Santa Nicklaus" by the Dutch. Over the years, the pronunciation changed to become "Sinterklaas" and then "Santa Claus."

continued...

Other nationalities brought their Christmas customs to North America as well. Soon, the Dutch began to celebrate the coming of Saint Nicholas, or Santa Claus, on Christmas Eve. The Germans, Italians, Swedes, and other nationalities adopted the Santa Claus tradition, too.

In 1809, the famous author Washington Irving wrote a story about New York and its Dutch settlers. In the story, he described a dream about Saint Nicholas in which the saint rode across the tree tops in a horse-drawn wagon. Irving's story made Saint Nicholas famous across the country.

The poet Clement Clarke Moore read Irving's story. It inspired him to write the now-famous poem that begins " 'Twas the night before Christmas." Moore was riding home in a sleigh filled with presents for his children when he got the idea for his poem. In his imagination, he saw Santa flying through the sky in a sleigh drawn by eight tiny reindeer. He described Santa as a plump, jolly, old elf. This description of Santa and his arrival on Christmas Eve became popular across the country. Moore's poem influenced our view of Santa forever.

In 1863, a cartoonist named Thomas Nast drew a picture of Santa Claus. It became so popular that he continued to do more drawings each year. Nast drew Santa as a jolly, bearded man in a fur-trimmed red suit. He also drew pictures of Santa's workshop, Santa's records of good and bad children, and Santa's home at the North Pole.

Today, we see Santa's helpers dressed in red suits and white beards on street corners and at shopping malls. But we all have our own special ideas about what Santa really looks like. The jolly gift-giver remains one of the best mysteries and best surprises of Christmas.

Ho-Ho-Ho's

How do Santa and Mrs. Claus pass the long winter nights at the North Pole?

They play Christmas cards.

What does Santa say while he works in his garden?

Hoe, hoe, hoe!

Where do Dancer, Dasher, Prancer, Comet, Cupid, Donder, and Blitzen come before Rudolph?

In the dictionary

Why does Santa Claus wear red suspenders?

To keep his pants up

What is filled every morning and emptied every night, except at Christmas when it is filled at night and emptied in the morning?

A stocking

What do astronauts get for Christmas?

Mistletoe

What Christmas message is in the following letters?
A B C D E F G H I J K M N O P Q R S T U V W X Y Z

Noel (No L)

Feliz Navidad

In Mexico, the Christmas greeting is "Feliz Navidad," Spanish for "Merry Christmas." A favorite Mexican decoration is this woven ornament. It is simple to make, but beautiful to hang from your tree.

Materials

Craft sticks (or thick twigs)   Scissors
Red and green yarn   Ruler

Steps

1. Cut a piece of yarn about 20 inches long. Cross two craft sticks or twigs in the center. Hold them together with one hand.

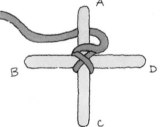

2. Wrap one end of the red yarn around the center of the two sticks several times. Tie a knot in it to secure the sticks in a cross shape.

3. Bring the yarn over arm A of the cross and then down under it.

4. Work counterclockwise around the cross. Bring the yarn under arm B, around, and over it.

5. Bring the yarn under arm C, around, and over it.

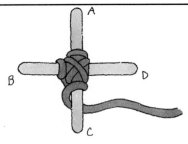

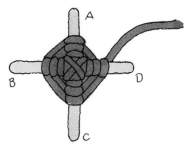

6. Bring the yarn under arm D, around, and over it.

7. Continue these steps around the cross. Wind each new turn of yarn next to the last one on the arm. Always work toward the ends of each arm.

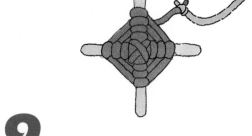

8. When a third of the arms are covered, change to green yarn. Knot the ends of the yarn pieces together to start the new color. After two-thirds of the arms are finished, change colors again. Besides green and red, you can use any colors or patterns you want for your designs.

9. When the arms are filled up, tie off the yarn in a knot around the last arm you did. Bring a length of the yarn up to use as a hanger.

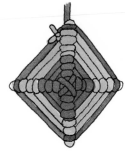

10. Hang your ornament on the Christmas tree. *Feliz Navidad.*

Santa Piñata

Mexican children celebrate Christmas with a colorful *piñata* full of candies and treats. The piñata is hung from the ceiling and then hit with a stick until it bursts open, showering everyone with candy. You can make this piñata and fill it with surprises for your friends.

Materials

Large, round balloon
White glue
Newspaper
Water
Scissors
Masking tape

Cotton balls or polyester fiberfill
Tempera or poster paint
Paintbrushes
Strong cord
Small gifts and candies
Bowl

Steps

1. Blow up the balloon, or have an adult help you, and tie off the end in a knot.

2. Make a mixture of white glue and water and put it in a shallow bowl. Cut newspaper into strips about one inch wide. Dip the strips into the glue. Paste the paper onto the balloon.

3. Cover the balloon with four layers of paper. Let the knot on top stick out to use later for hanging. Smooth down the strips of paper as you work and wipe off any excess paste. Let the balloon dry overnight.

4. When dry, cut a small hole (about one inch in diameter) in the bottom of the piñata. Fill the balloon with small candies and gifts. Tape the hole shut with masking tape.

5. Paint Santa's face on the piñata. Use pink paint for the face; red paint for the hat, cheeks, and mouth; blue paint for the eyes; and white paint for the hat's trim.

continued...

6. Paste cotton balls or fiberfill onto the piñata for Santa's beard.

7. Attach a heavy cord to the top of the piñata by tying it around the knot of the balloon.

8. Your piñata is ready to hang. The custom in Mexico is to blindfold a child and let him or her try to hit the piñata with a stick to break it open. You can play this game most safely with a lightweight, plastic bat. When someone breaks the piñata, everybody is a winner. *Feliz Navidad.*

Rudolph and Friends

Can you remember the names of Santa's eight tiny reindeer? They are: Dasher, Dancer, Prancer, Vixen, Comet, Cupid, Donder, and Blitzen.

But who is the most famous reindeer of all? Rudolph the Red-Nosed Reindeer. Despite his fame, Rudolph is one of our newest Christmas legends. He first appeared in 1939.

Rudolph was first imagined by Robert L. May, who wrote advertisements for Montgomery Ward & Company. May was hired to write a little book to give to the children who visited Santa at the Montgomery Ward stores. In the book, an "ugly duckling" reindeer named Rudolph saved Christmas for Santa by lighting up the foggy sky with his bright nose.

In 1949, Gene Autry, the singing cowboy, recorded the now-famous song about Rudolph. Today, Rudolph stars in movies, cartoons, and books. Nobody laughs at Rudolph anymore or calls him names. He's gone down in history!

Reindeer Facts

Did You Know?

Real reindeer don't live at the North Pole. Their habitat is the snowy regions of northern Europe and Asia. The animals live in large herds that migrate from place to place, seeking new feeding grounds.

The North American relative of the reindeer is the caribou. Each spring, caribou head north across the wide, treeless tundra of the arctic region, feeding on the low-growing mosses and lichens that grow there. In the fall, the caribou head back south to where food can be found in the winter.

Both male and female reindeer have antlers. They stand about three and a half feet tall and weigh about three hundred pounds.

The feet of reindeer and caribou are well adapted to their climate. Each foot has hooved toes that grip ice and spread out on snow to prevent the deer from sinking in.

Like Rudolph, a real reindeer or caribou has a special nose. Its keen sense of smell can help the animal locate plants under a deep cover of snow. The animal's large nostrils warm the frigid air before it reaches the lungs.

In northern Scandinavia, people called the Lapps are reindeer herders. For centuries, they have migrated with the reindeer, as the animals search for new grazing land. The Lapps use the reindeer meat for food, their skins for clothing, and their bones and antlers for tools.

Santa's Science

To make these Christmas gifts, Santa moves out of the workshop and into the laboratory. Each gift is based on a simple scientific experiment that you can do at home. When you give the gift, explain the science ideas that helped you to make it.

Shiny Pennies

A gift of shiny Christmas pennies is perfect for brothers, sisters, cousins, and friends. You don't have to go to the bank for new copper coins. You can transform old, dirty pennies into shiny, new ones with this simple experiment.

Materials

1 tablespoon salt
3 tablespoons white vinegar
Dirty pennies
Water

Small glass jar
Measuring spoons
Towel

Steps

1. Pour the white vinegar into the jar. Add the salt.

2. Drop approximately 10 dirty pennies into the jar. Let them sit in the liquid for several minutes.

3. Remove the pennies, rinse them with water, and dry them with a towel.

4. Repeat Steps 2 and 3 for more pennies. Repeat Step 1 to make a clean mixture, if needed.

5. Perform this magic science trick on Christmas day for your family. It's an experiment worth watching.

Why It Happens

When you combine the salt and vinegar, you have made a weak form of hydrochloric acid. The chemical name for vinegar is acetic acid; table salt is sodium chloride. Mixed together, they create an acid that can clean dirt and tarnish off copper.

Electronic Quiz Board

This gift is a bit complicated to make. But the results are worth it! By using electric circuits, you can make a question-and-answer board that lights up every time the player gives the correct answer. It's a gift that is sure to light up someone's Christmas.

Materials

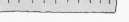

17 feet of bell wire (from a hardware or hobby store)
Flashlight bulb and socket (from a hobby store)
1 1/2-volt dry-cell battery
Heavy cardboard rectangle, 12 x 15 inches
Screwdriver
White paper

Ruler
Scissors
Pencil or marker
Clear tape
Nail or pushpin

Steps

1. Use a pencil and ruler to mark 20 dots on a piece of cardboard, as shown in the illustration. The first mark on each side is made three inches from the top and one inch from the left or right side. The remaining nine marks on each side are one inch apart. Using a nail or a pushpin, punch small holes through all 20 marks.

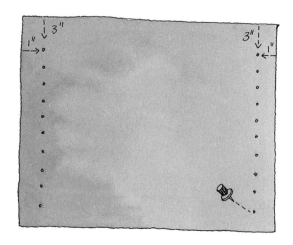

2. Number the holes on the right 1 to 10, beginning at the top. Number the holes on the left in this order from the top: 8 4 6 1 9 2 10 3 5 7.

3. Cut the bell wire into 13 pieces of about 15 inches each. Bare one inch of wire on both ends of each piece. Push the end of one wire through hole #1 on the right side. Tie a knot on the other side to keep it in place. Push the other end of the same wire through hole #1 on the left side. Tie a knot on the other side of the board. Repeat, matching the numbers for the remaining nine sets of holes.

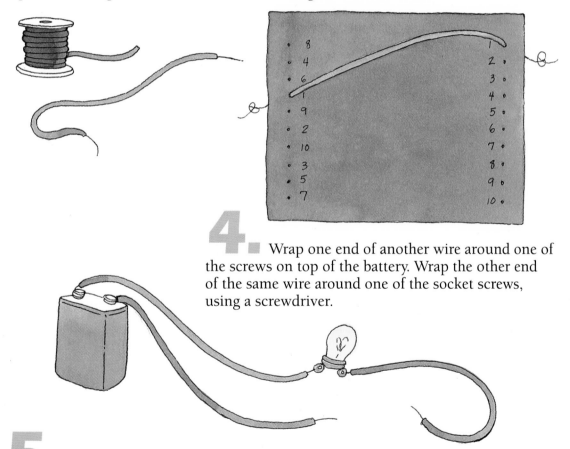

4. Wrap one end of another wire around one of the screws on top of the battery. Wrap the other end of the same wire around one of the socket screws, using a screwdriver.

5. Connect one of the remaining wires to the other battery screw. Connect the last wire to the other socket screw. (Two of the wires now have free ends.)

continued...

6. Cut a large piece of white paper to fit the front of the board in between the loops of wire. Write 10 questions down the left side, one beside each hole. Write the 10 answers to your questions down the right side in this order: 8 4 6 1 9 2 10 3 5 7. Tape the paper to the front of the board.

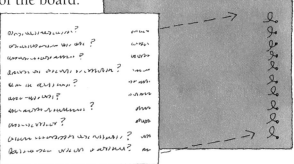

7. Pick up the free ends of the battery and socket wires. Touch the end of the battery wire to the knot beside a question and the end of the socket wire to your answer. If you are correct, the bulb will light up!

8. Make up a question-and-answer sheet for everyone in your family. Preschoolers can match letters and pictures. Older family and friends can answer trivia questions and match facts.

Why It Happens

When you match a question and answer correctly, you connect the wires to form a complete path, or circuit. Electricity is able to flow from the battery through the wire behind the board to the bulb, causing it to light up.

Gingerbread Men

Gingerbread men are Christmas classics. They are fun to make, delicious to eat, and charming to hang on the tree. You can use a cookie cutter in the shape of a gingerbread man with this recipe. Or if you don't have one, trace your own design onto a piece of paper. Then transfer it to a piece of cardboard. Cut out the cardboard design. Place your pattern on the rolled-out cookie dough. Use a small butter knife to cut your cookie dough.

You Will Need

1/2 cup light molasses
1/4 cup granulated sugar
3 tablespoons butter or margarine
1 tablespoon milk
2 cups flour
1/2 teaspoon baking soda
1/2 teaspoon salt
1/2 teaspoon each: nutmeg, cinnamon, powdered cloves, and ginger
Measuring cup and spoons

Small and large mixing bowls
Mixing spoon
Sifter
Rolling pin
Floured wooden cutting board
Greased cookie sheet
Potholder
Spatula
Cookie cutter (or pattern and butter knife)
Optional: raisins, small red candies

Steps

1. Cream the butter in a large mixing bowl. Add light molasses, sugar, and milk to butter. Mix until smooth.

2. Sift together flour, baking soda, salt, cinnamon, nutmeg, ground cloves, and ginger in a small bowl.

31

continued...

3. Pour half the flour mixture into the large bowl. Stir until well mixed. Add the remaining flour mixture. Flour your hands and mix the ingredients well by hand. If the dough seems too dry, add up to 2 tablespoons of water.

4. Grease the cookie sheet and preheat the oven to 350°F. If you're not allowed to use the oven by yourself, ask an adult for help.

5. Put one quarter of the dough onto the floured cutting board or a floured kitchen counter. Refrigerate remaining dough until ready to use. Flour the rolling pin, then roll out the dough evenly to one-eighth inch thickness.

FLOUR

6. Use a cookie cutter (or a butter knife and the pattern) to cut out the gingerbread men. Use a spatula to lift them onto the cookie sheet.

7. Before baking, add raisin eyes and buttons to the gingerbread men. Add a red candy mouth, if you like.

8. Bake 10 minutes, or until light brown around the edges. Use a potholder to take the pan out of the oven. Let cookies cool on the sheet for several minutes; then remove with a spatula.

9. Enjoy eating your merry gingerbread men.

Christmas Secrets

Christmas is a time for secrets. You want to know what presents you're being given. And everybody else wants to know what you're giving them.

A secret code can come in handy at a time like this. You can write your shopping list in code. You can write top-secret messages to friends or brothers and sisters.

There are many different ways to write a code. You have to create your own system so that no one can crack it easily. To write in code is called encoding. To break the code is called decoding.

Here are some examples of encoding that you can use for your Christmas code.

NFSSZ DISJTUNBT

Can you decode this holiday message? Have you given up? It says: MERRY CHRISTMAS. Look at the message carefully again and see if you can break the code.

The code uses simple letter substitution. Each letter in MERRY CHRISTMAS is substituted by the letter that follows it in the alphabet. Simple, but tricky!

YPPA HXSY ADIL OH

Try to decode this message. Want a hint? You read the words often at Christmas time.

The message says: HAPPY HOLIDAYS. Before reading how the code was made, see if you can break it.

The code uses letter reversal and a special code letter to signal the end of a word. The letters are also split into groups of four rather than grouped by word. The words HAPPY HOLIDAYS are spelled backwards. The code letter X is put in between the words. Then the message is broken into sections of four letters each.

Trickier yet!

4–5–1–18   19–1–14–20–1

What could these strange numbers mean?

The message reads: DEAR SANTA. Try to break the code. Numbers were substituted for the letters of the alphabet in this example. The letters A through Z were given the numbers 1 through 26. It's simple, if you know the trick!

You can have lots of fun making a Christmas code. If you are sharing it with a friend, be sure you both understand the rules of the code. And as Santa would say, OHXO HXOH.

Joyeux Noël

In France, the Christmas cracker is an old holiday tradition. The cracker is a paper tube filled with candy. Two children tug at the ends until the paper "cracks" open, and out spills the candy.

Follow the directions below for making Christmas crackers for your family and friends. When you give them as gifts, wish everyone a "Joyeux Noël." It means "Merry Christmas" in French.

Materials

Gold-foil or silver-foil gift wrap
Brightly wrapped candies
Clear tape

Ribbons
Scissors
Ruler

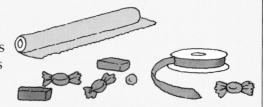

Steps

1. Cut the foil paper into sheets that are approximately 8 inches wide by 12 inches long. Bring the 12-inch sides together, overlapping them about half an inch. Tape the edges together, but do not crease the tube you've made.

2. Stuff about 10 candies into the middle of the hollow tube. The number of candies you use will depend on their size.

3. Measure three inches in from both ends of the cracker. Twist the ends at this point and tie off each end with a piece of ribbon. Arrange the paper at both ends so it flares out. Holding the ends, push in a little to make your cracker puff up.

4. To make your cracker "crack," pull on one end while someone else pulls on the other. Your tug-of-war will finally burst open the cracker. Enjoy the candy. And *Joyeux Noël*.

A Christmas Lantern

All around the world, people light candles at Christmas. The flickering light symbolizes joy and new life. With a few simple materials, you can make a special lantern to light up Christmas at your home. Early American tinsmiths made lanterns like these, and children in Mexico still do.

Materials

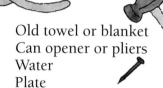

Tin can of any size
Hammer
Nail
Short, thick candle

Old towel or blanket
Can opener or pliers
Water
Plate

Steps

1. Remove the lid from a used tin can. Smooth down any sharp edges with a can opener or pliers. Wash and dry the can.

2. Fill the can with water and put it in the freezer. Take it out when the water has turned to ice.

3. Fold an old towel and lay it on the floor. Put the can down on its side on the towel.

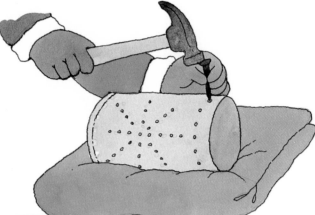

4. Ask an adult to help you use a hammer and nail to punch holes in the can. Follow the design shown here. Or create your own design. Try to make holes on all sides of the can. Leave at least half an inch from the bottom without holes so melted wax won't drip out later.

5. Place the can in the sink and let the ice melt. Dry the can. With an adult's help, drip a little melted wax into the bottom of the can, then press the candle into it.

6. Set your lantern on a plate or heatproof surface. When the candle is lit, the design will flicker joyfully throughout your house.

Fortune Nuts

This Christmas, give your family a nutty surprise. Like fortune cookies, these fortune nuts predict the future. Hang them from your Christmas tree as ornaments. On Christmas day, ask everybody to choose a nut from the tree. When they crack it open, they'll learn their future in a nutshell.

Materials

Walnuts	Pen or pencil
Knife	Glue
Narrow strips of paper, each about 4 inches long	Red yarn or ribbon
	Scissors

Steps

1. Ask an adult to help you split open each walnut along the seam in its shell. You should end up with two equal halves of the shell.

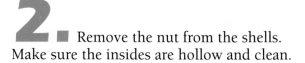

2. Remove the nut from the shells. Make sure the insides are hollow and clean.

3. Write out fortunes on the narrow strips of paper. These can be humorous sayings, wise predictions, or family jokes.

4. Roll up the paper with the fortune on it and put it inside one of the shells.

5. Cut yarn or ribbon into six-inch lengths. Knot one end and lay the knot inside the shell on the rounded end of the walnut.

6. Take the other side of the same shell and dot glue around the edges. Press the two halves of the shell together.

7. When dry, hang the fortune nuts on your tree. Nuts are a traditional Christmas decoration. These nuts may become a tradition in your family.

Family Taffy Pull

This family project will *pull* everyone together at Christmas time. The recipe is for molasses taffy, a sweet treat that's fun to make. Before the taffy hardens, it has to be pulled into a long rope by two people. Remember, you must have adult help to make this recipe.

You Will Need

2 cups white, granulated sugar
1 cup light molasses
1/4 cup water
2 teaspoons vinegar
2 tablespoons butter, plus enough to grease pans, hands, and scissors
1/2 teaspoon vanilla
1/2 teaspoon baking soda
Candy thermometer (or a glass of very cold water)

Wooden spoon
Large saucepan
Cookie sheet
Spatula
Large plate or platter
Scissors
Plastic wrap
Potholder
Measuring spoons and cup

Steps

1. To begin, grease a large cookie sheet with butter or margarine. Set it aside to use later.

2. Now butter the sides of a large saucepan. Combine sugar, light molasses, and water in the saucepan. Attach the candy thermometer to the side of the pan.

3. Ask an adult to help you stir the mixture over medium heat until the sugar dissolves. Bring to a boil; then add the vinegar. Cook to 270°F. If you don't have a candy thermometer, drop a bit of syrup into a glass of cold water. When the syrup forms a hard ball, it is hot enough.

4. Using a potholder, remove the pan from heat. Mix in butter, baking soda, and vanilla. Stir well.

5. Ask an adult to help you pour the taffy onto a greased cookie sheet. Don't scrape what stays in the saucepan. Let the taffy cool. You can use a spatula to turn the edges into the center for even cooling. Wait until taffy is still warm, but not too hot to handle.

43

continued...

6. Grease your hands with butter. Pick up the taffy and pull it into a long rope. Double up the rope and twist it. Pull again. Repeat until taffy turns a golden color and becomes hard. Pull it out into a rope about half an inch thick. Quickly go to the next step.

7. Rub butter on a pair of scissors. Cut the taffy rope into pieces about one inch long. Let them fall onto the large plate.

8. Wrap each piece of taffy in clear plastic. You'll agree that the work was worth it.

Trivia Quiz

1. What is the name of the Christmas flower?

2. What is Ebenezer Scrooge famous for? Who created him?

3. What does the word Noël mean in "The First Noël"?

4. What famous event in American history took place on Christmas in 1776?

5. What is a yule log?

6. What does it mean if Santa Claus leaves an apple in the toe of your Christmas stocking and an orange in the heel?

7. What small American town has the world's largest statue of Santa Claus?

8. What famous ballet is performed at Christmas time?

Answers to Trivia Quiz

1. The poinsettia is the traditional Christmas flower. It was named after Dr. Joel Poinsett, the first U.S. ambassador to Mexico. He brought the flower from Mexico to the United States.

2. Ebenezer Scrooge is the man who hated Christmas and was too stingy to give presents. He was the creation of writer Charles Dickens in *A Christmas Carol*.

3. *Noël* is the French word for "Christmas." It is also used to mean a Christmas carol.

4. On Christmas in 1776, George Washington led his troops across the Delaware River to attack the British at their headquarters in Trenton, New Jersey. The surprise attack turned the tide of the American Revolution in favor of the colonists.

5. A yule log is a large piece of firewood, which is burned on Christmas Eve. It is said to bring light and warmth, hope and good fortune into a house.

6. According to tradition, the apple is for good luck and the orange is a reward for being good.

7. The town of Santa Claus, Indiana, has a statue of Santa that is 23 feet tall.

8. The ballet is the *The Nutcracker*. The great Russian composer, Peter Ilich Tchaikovsky, wrote the music for the ballet.

Merry Christmas!

MUSCLES

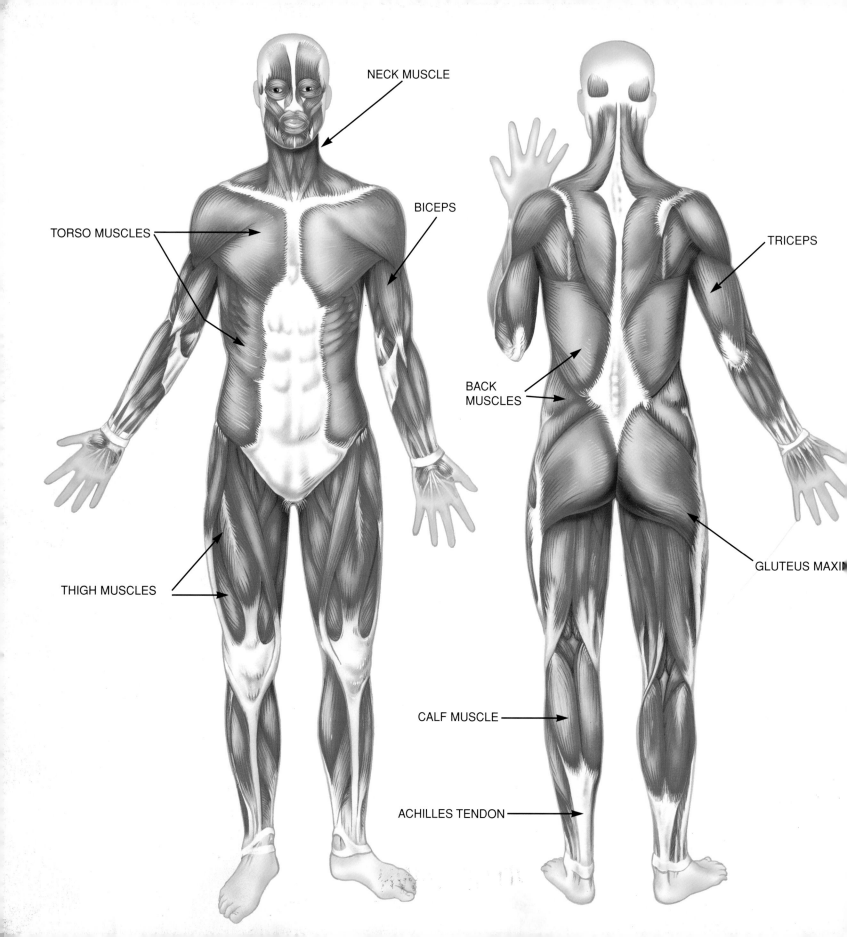

NECK MUSCLE

BICEPS

TORSO MUSCLES

TRICEPS

BACK
MUSCLES

GLUTEUS MAXI

THIGH MUSCLES

CALF MUSCLE

ACHILLES TENDON

MUSCLES

OUR MUSCULAR SYSTEM

SEYMOUR SIMON

HarperCollins*Publishers*

PHOTOGRAPHY NOTE

Scientists are using fantastic new machines that peer inside the human body to picture the invisible and help doctors save lives. In this book, we see extraordinary views of the interior of the human body. Many of these images were taken by various kinds of scanners, which change X-ray photos into computer code to make clear, colorful graphics. The computer-enhanced pictures of planets beamed back to Earth from distant space use a similar technique. These new ways of seeing help all of us to understand and appreciate that most wonderful machine: the human body.

The author would like to thank Orli R. Etingin, M.D., for her careful
reading of the manuscript of this book.

PHOTO AND ART CREDITS

Permission to use the following photographs is gratefully acknowledged: page 7, John Daugherty/Photo Researchers, Inc.;
page 11, P. Motta/University La Sapienza, Rome/Science Photo Library; pages 12, 15, VU/David M. Phillips; page 13, VU/Triarch;
page 14, VU/Fred Hossler; page 17, Jean-Loup Charmet/Science Photo Library; pages 19, 23, 29, 31, Scott Camazine;
page 20, John Bavosi/Science Photo Library; pages 24, 26–27, 32, Tim Davis/Photo Researchers, Inc.
Art on pages 2 and 8 by Ann Neumann.

Library of Congress Cataloging-in-Publication Data
Simon, Seymour.
   Muscles: our muscular system / Seymour Simon.
     p.   cm.
   Summary: Describes the nature and work of muscles, the different kinds, and the effects of exercise and other activities on them.
   ISBN 0-688-14642-2 (trade) — ISBN 0-688-14643-0 (lib. bdg.) — ISBN 0-688-17720-4 (pbk.)
   1. Muscles—Juvenile literature.   [1. Muscles.   2. Muscular system.]   I. Title.
QP321.S4858   1998   97-44758
612.7'4—dc21   CIP
                                                                     AC

❖
Visit us on the World Wide Web! www.harperchildrens.com

To the editors and designers
at Morrow Junior Books,
who helped create this series

Whenever you walk or run, play an instrument, or turn a page of a book, muscles move your body. Even when you're still, muscles are at work, moving your eyelids each time you blink and moving your chest in and out each time you breathe. Your muscles are always moving, even when you are fast asleep.

Muscles make up about 40 percent of a normal person's body weight. Fat, by contrast, makes up only about 10 percent. In addition to the 640 muscles that you control, such as your arm and leg muscles, there are many muscles that you *don't* control. Among these are your stomach muscles, which aid the digestion of your food, and your heart muscles, which keep blood pumping through your body.

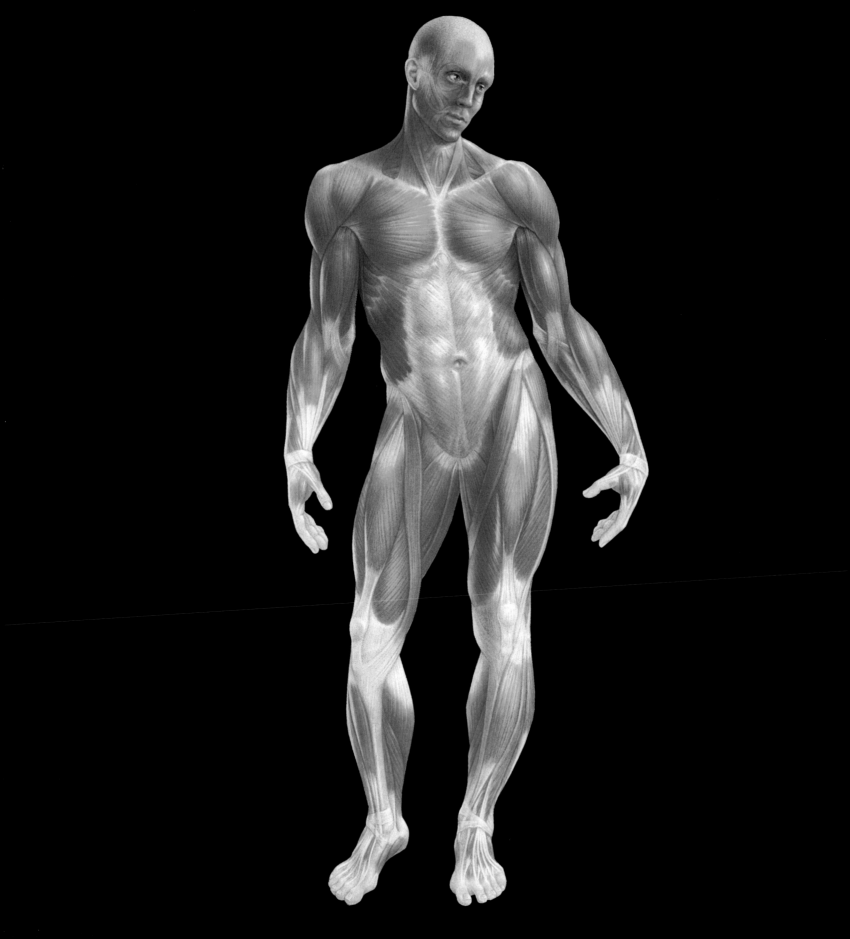

ARM STRAIGHT

ARM BENT

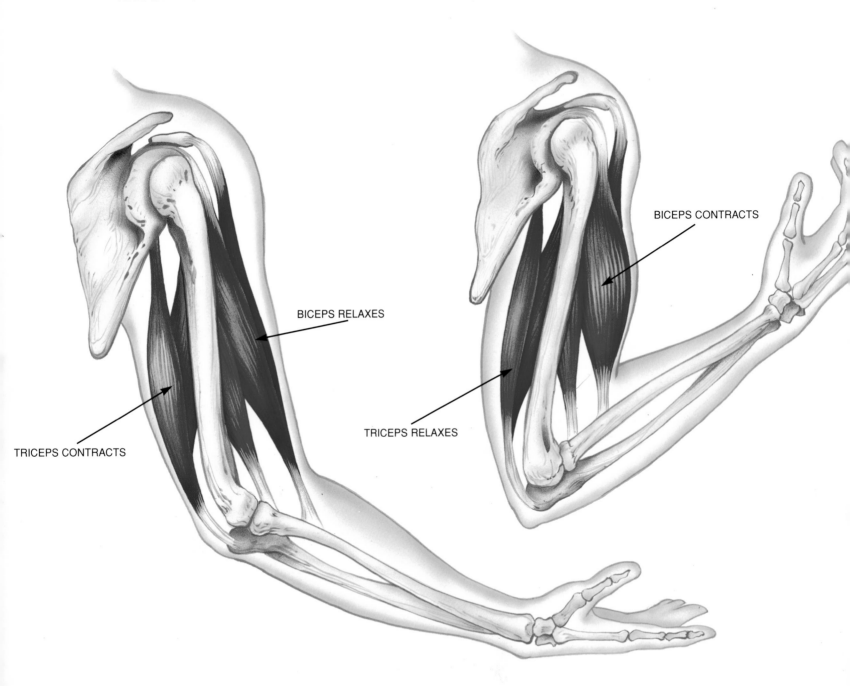

BICEPS CONTRACTS

BICEPS RELAXES

TRICEPS RELAXES

TRICEPS CONTRACTS

Muscles move your body by contracting. When a muscle contracts, it shortens, and that moves the bones to which it is attached. When a muscle relaxes, it lengthens or stretches. Muscles are usually arranged in pairs, so that while one muscle pulls the bone, another muscle relaxes. For instance, when you make a fist and bend your arm, your biceps muscle bends your elbow and your triceps muscle relaxes. Straightening out your arm again causes your triceps muscle to contract and your biceps muscle to relax.

Muscles are attached to bones by narrow, ropelike tissues called tendons. These tendons help to move the bone each time a muscle contracts. Flex your arm back and forth; you can feel the tendons and see them under your skin, moving like tight cords. You can easily see other muscle tendons along the sides of your neck and ankles and behind your knees.

Muscles are made up of bundles of long, thin cells called muscle fibers. A single muscle fiber is thinner than the finest human hair and can be up to a foot long in a large muscle. Despite its size, a muscle fiber is a single cell. Each muscle fiber is made up of thousands of even thinner threads called fibrils, and each fibril is made up of strands of two kinds of proteins, actin and myosin. Proteins are important chemicals that the body uses to make muscles, bones, skin, and other body parts.

Muscles are controlled by electrical signals that come into the muscles from nerves in the brain and spinal cord. When the muscle fibrils receive signals, the actin strands slide past the myosin strands, overlapping the way the teeth of two combs would if you put them together. This sliding action makes the muscle get shorter and thicker, and that moves the part of the body to which it is attached. When the actin strands slide in the other direction, the muscle gets longer and thinner, and it relaxes.

A blood vessel (blue) snakes along muscle fibers (pink).

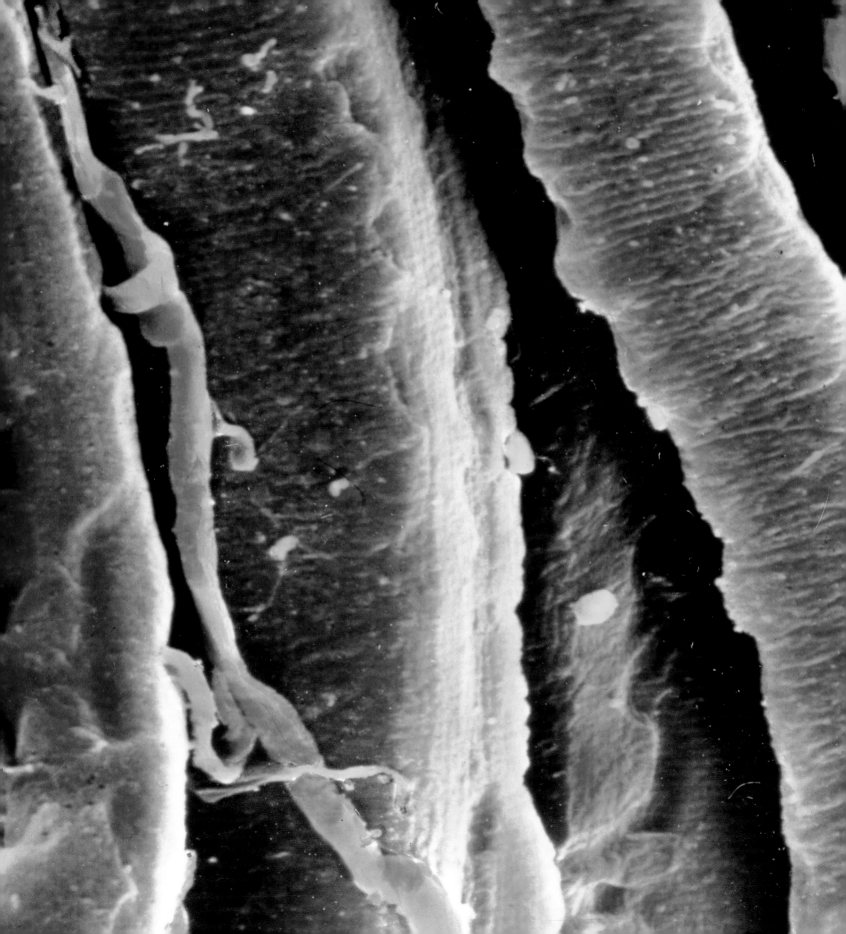

There are three kinds of muscles in the body. Muscles attached to bones are called skeletal muscles. Because you can control your skeletal muscles, they are also called voluntary muscles. These muscles look striped, or striated, under a microscope because the muscle fibers lie next to one another.

Another kind of muscle is called smooth muscle. It is also known as involuntary muscle, because you cannot consciously move it. Unlike skeletal muscles,

These images of skeletal muscle (left) and smooth muscle (right) have been magnified hundreds of times.

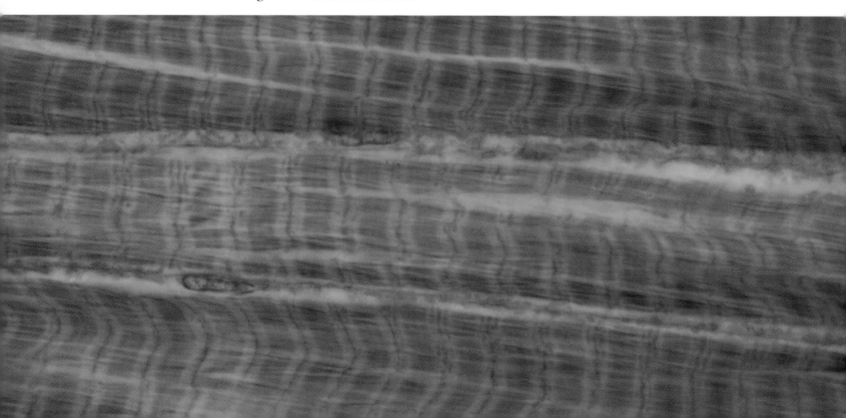

smooth muscles do not look striped under a micro-scope.

Smooth muscles line the walls of the stomach and the intestines and other hollow tubes, such as blood vessels. These muscles contract the way skeletal muscles do, only much more slowly, and they use less energy than skeletal muscles. As the muscles around the stomach and the intestines contract, they move food through the digestive system.

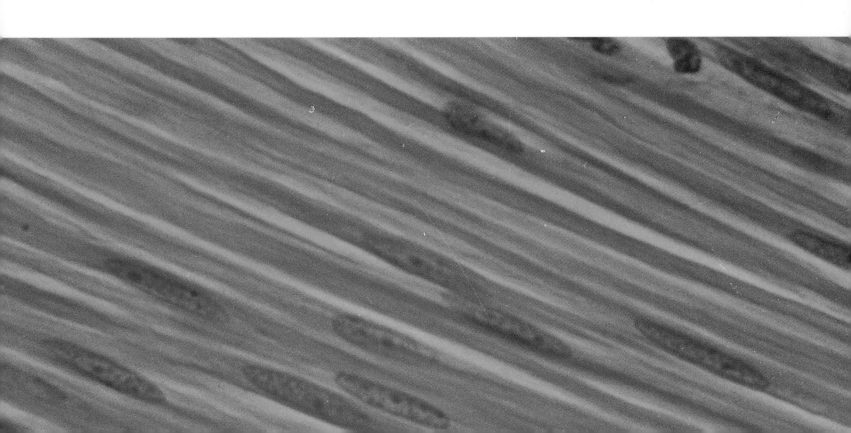

The heart is made of still another kind of muscle. This thick, powerful muscle is called heart, or cardiac, muscle. Cardiac muscle continually contracts and relaxes, pumping blood around your body sixty to seventy times a minute, one hundred thousand times a day. Cardiac muscle never tires, the way skeletal muscles do.

Like smooth muscle, cardiac muscle is involuntary; you cannot consciously make your heart muscles contract. Cardiac muscle has its own built-in rhythm of contracting and relaxing, but signals sent by the brain and nerves can change the rhythm, as can body chemicals called hormones.

Cardiac muscle (below and right) looks striped under a microscope, something like skeletal muscle.

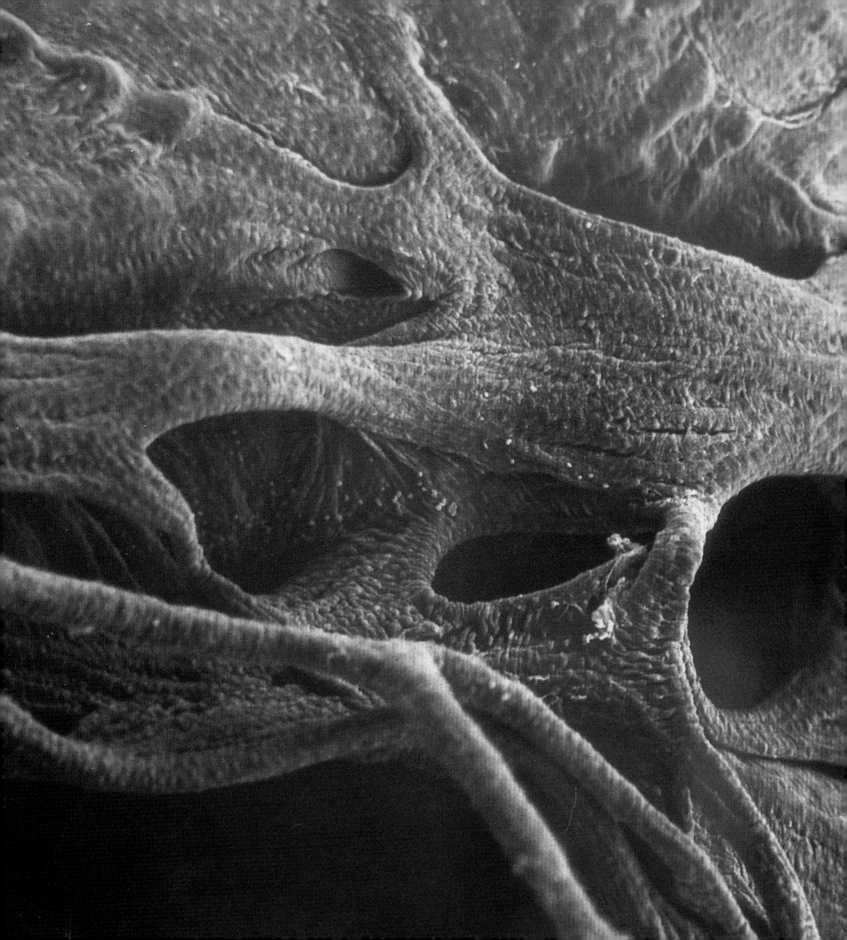

Your face and neck have more than thirty different sets of muscles. Most of them are small and are attached to each other or to the skin, rather than to bones. You use certain muscles to express your moods: When two muscles pull up the corners of your mouth, you smile; if other muscles raise your eyebrows, you look surprised.

Powerful muscles in your cheeks and at the side of your head move your jaw when you speak or eat. Another group of muscles moves the lips in many different directions. The muscles of the lips, together with the tongue and the vocal cords in your throat, produce the many movements and sounds needed for speech.

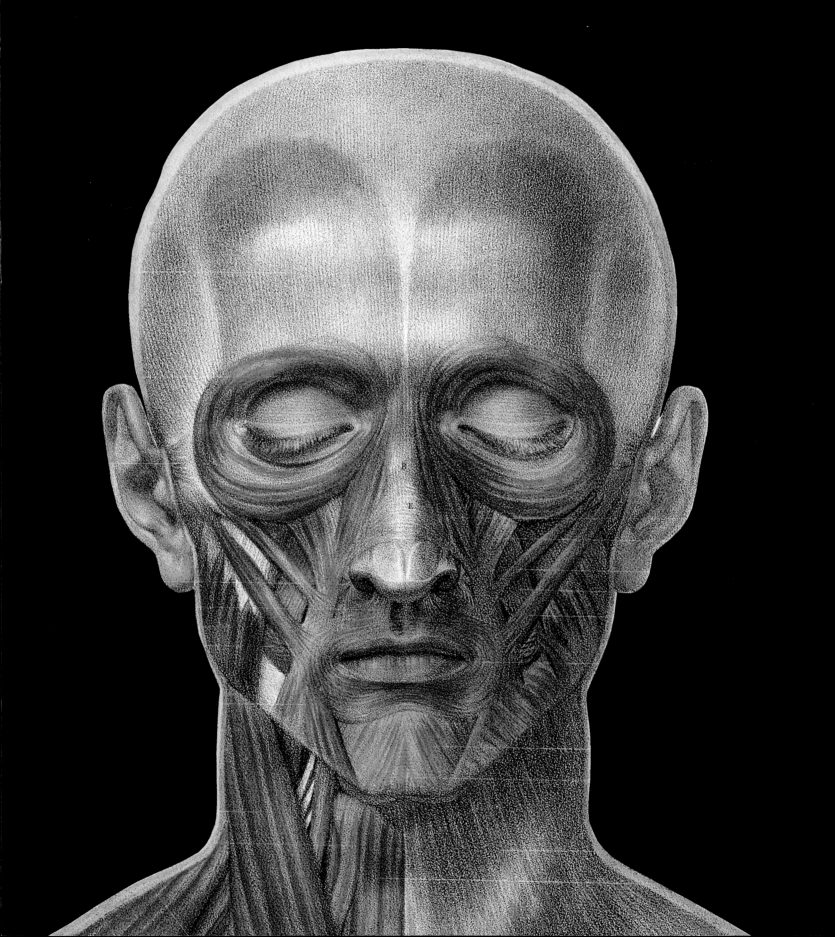

Layers of different muscles surround the central part of your body, which is called the trunk or the torso. The torso contains the heart and lungs and other important organs. Dozens of torso muscles help you to move and breathe and allow you to twist and turn.

Powerful pairs of muscles in your back are an important part of your torso. These help you to stay upright. Other muscle pairs in the front of your torso move your arms and shoulders.

A strong muscle called the diaphragm stretches across your torso from the backbone to the ribs. The diaphragm moves up and down as you breathe in and out. At the same time, muscles between your ribs and diaphragm move your ribs outward and inward as air pushes into and out of your lungs.

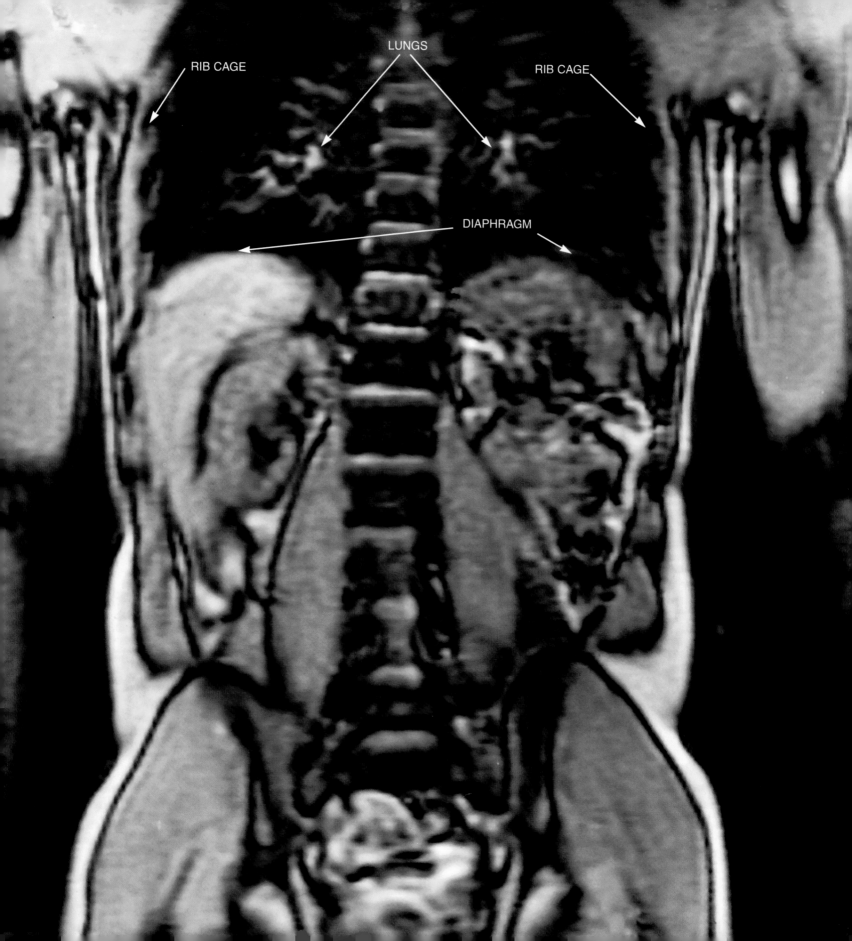

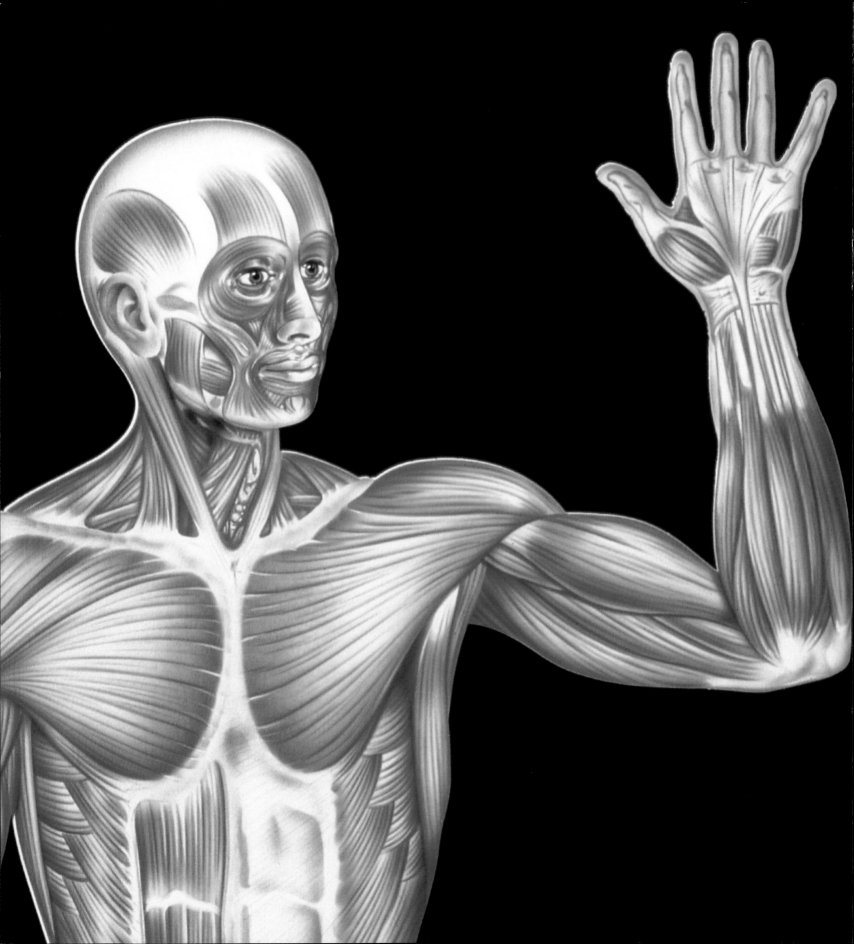

The muscles of your hands and arms work together like a set of delicate tools at the end of a powerful machine. Together, these muscles can gently pick up a tiny feather, or they can support your weight when you do a handstand.

The biceps and triceps bend or straighten the arm and turn it around. When you flex your arm to "make a muscle," the biceps bulge out. There are nineteen muscles in your lower arm and twenty muscles in your hand that control your fingers and your wrist.

The thumb is the most movable part of the hand. Four muscles in your forearm and four in your hand control your thumb and allow you to hold things easily.

The largest and strongest skeletal muscles in your body are in your legs. They help you walk and run, squat down or stand on tiptoes, and they keep you steady when you stand still.

The strong calf muscle at the back of the lower leg makes the foot bend forward and also helps to bend the knee. It is connected to the heel bone by the Achilles tendon, the strongest tendon in the body. The muscles in your feet and toes are like those in your hands and fingers, but the foot muscles are stronger and less flexible.

The biggest muscle in the body, the gluteus maximus in the buttocks, helps to flex the thighs. Other strong muscle pairs in your thighs provide the power to straighten your knees and to swivel your hips each time you stand, walk, run, leap, climb stairs, or sit down.

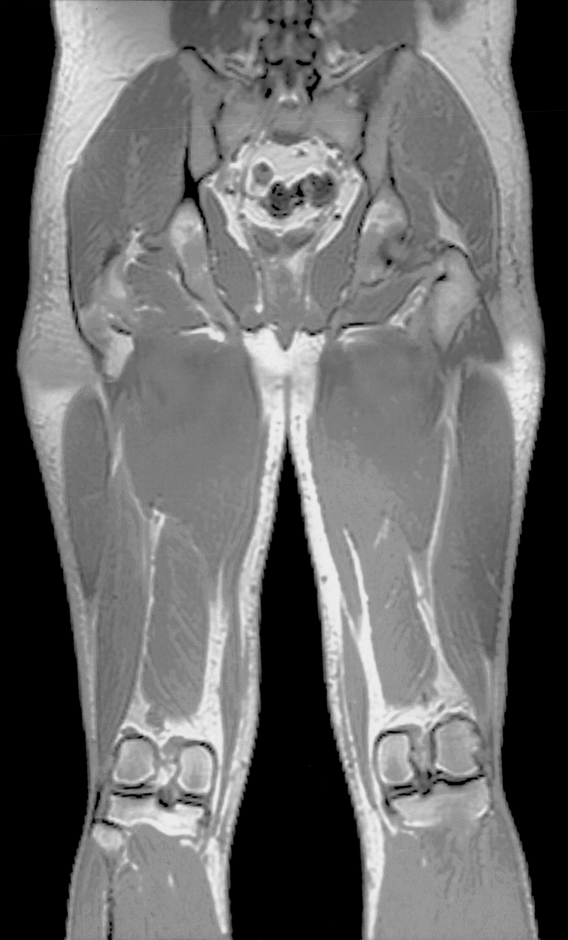

Muscles need food and oxygen in order to work properly. The chemicals in foods build muscle cells and help to repair them if they are damaged. Oxygen, which is carried by red blood cells, enters your muscles and allows you to exercise for long periods of time. The harder your muscles work, the more oxygen they need.

The more a muscle is exercised, the larger the muscle cells become. The blood vessels that enter the muscle widen so that more needed food and oxygen can be supplied. You can use well-exercised muscles for a longer time without tiring them.

Exercise doesn't give you more muscles, but it strengthens the muscles you have and helps keep them working well. Without exercise, muscles shrink and tire easily. This can happen if you are ill and unable to exercise for a long time.

Most athletes like to stretch or warm up their muscles before they compete in a sporting event. Muscles use oxygen and release energy when they are used. This is why you feel hot when you exercise. A warm muscle contracts more quickly and easily, receives more oxygen, and can perform for a longer time than a cold one. Stretching or warming up a muscle can help to prevent injury.

Depending upon the sport, different muscles are used in a warm-up. Runners may stretch out their calf muscles and do some light jogging with brief bursts of speed, while tennis players may stretch their back and arm muscles by hitting a ball easily and without too much power.

Exercise makes all muscles tired, even strong ones. Clench your fingers and open them again. If you continue to do this rapidly for several minutes, you will eventually have to stop as your muscles tire. That's because your arm and hand muscles are using up oxygen faster than your body can supply it. When this happens, a waste product called lactic acid builds up in the muscle, causing it to tighten or cramp. This can be very painful. The lactic acid usually breaks down in minutes as the muscle rests.

Sometimes muscles begin to hurt because they are strained. A strain usually results from too much use of a muscle, which can tear muscle fibers and cause pain.

Lifting too heavy an object can cause a sudden painful strain in lower back muscles. Cold ice packs on the strain can numb the pain that often follows. A strain is not the same as a sprain, which happens when you injure a joint, such as your ankle or elbow.

This MRI scan shows muscles (pink and red) around the stomach and lower chest.
The kidneys (purple) are to the top left and right.

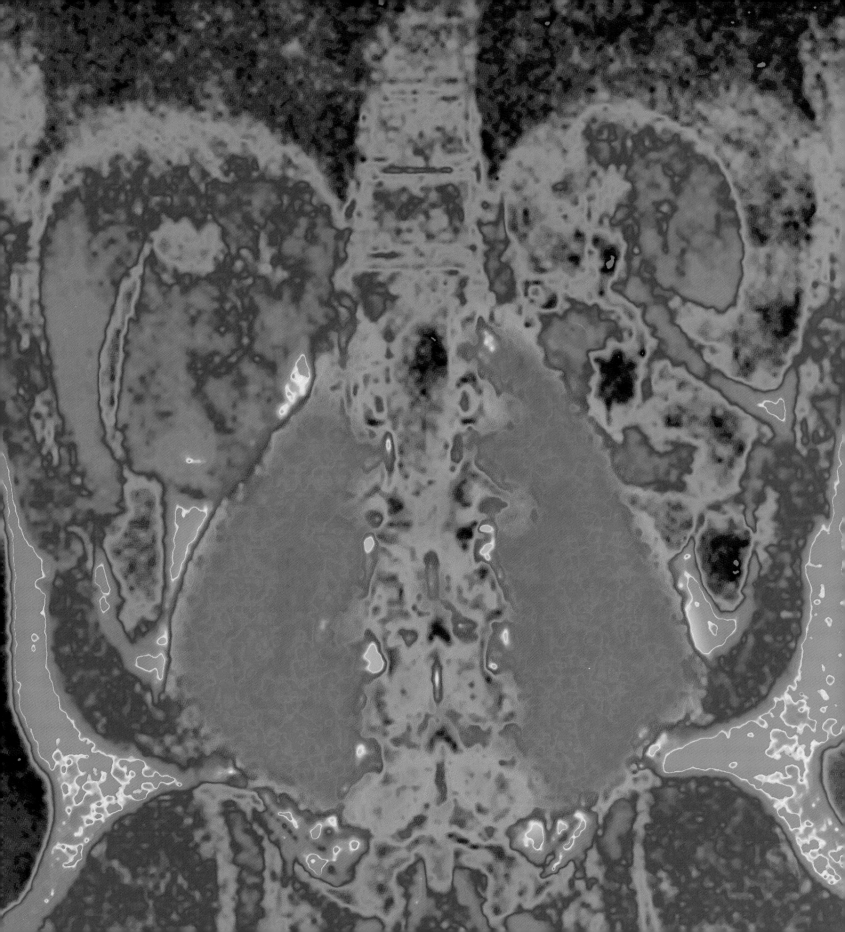

When a muscle is injured, doctors can often look at it without having to perform surgery. New ways of viewing the muscles and the bones help doctors understand what's going on inside the body. Computerized axial tomography (CAT) scans process dozens of X-ray pictures with computers to produce three-dimensional images of muscles and bones. Magnetic resonance imaging, or MRI, scans use powerful magnetic fields that are deflected by tissues that contain a lot of water. Bones don't contain much water, so they do not appear in an MRI, but the surrounding muscles appear very clearly in color images produced by computers.

Other imaging techniques, called SPECT and PET, use radioactive chemicals to show whether muscle tissues are getting enough blood. A test called an EMG measures electrical output and is used to test nerve damage in a muscle.

CAT scan of head

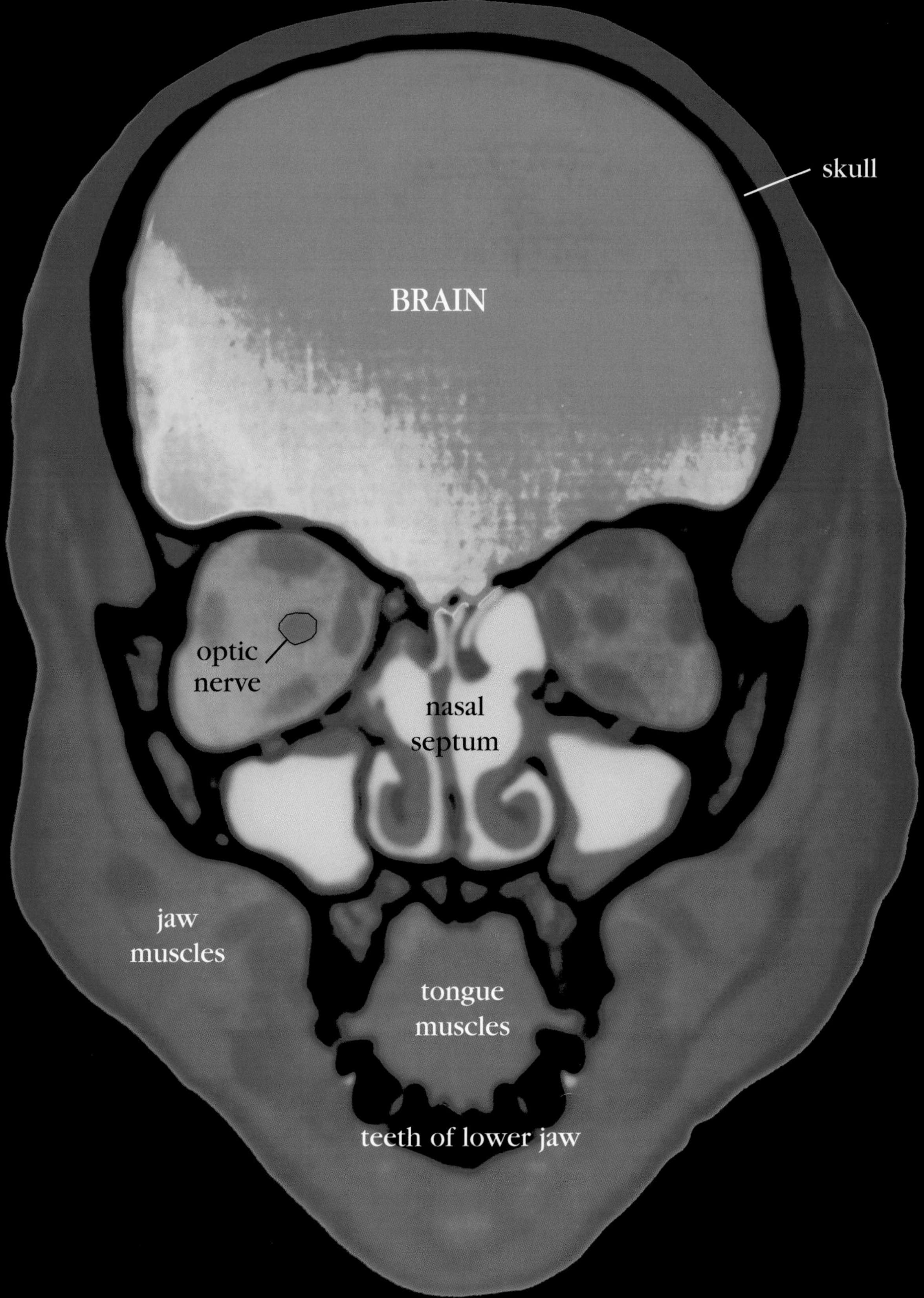

skull

BRAIN

optic nerve

nasal septum

jaw muscles

tongue muscles

teeth of lower jaw

Your muscles adjust themselves to your own movements and activities. There are muscles that you control, and muscles, like those in your heart, that work without your even knowing it. Muscles and bones work together every minute of the day, year after year, to keep your body moving and alive.